CONCERNS OF A CURIOUS MIND

PER ASPRA, AD ASTRA

MALIK AAQIB

To My Loving Grandfather;
Haji Abdul Subhan Malik

Contents

Foreword

By: Dr. Craig Shiner

"Concerns Of A Curious Mind" is a beautifully written book that offers insights into different scientific concepts. The author of the book is a good friend and a colleague of mine. Although very younger than me, he is gifted intellectually. I first got to know him through his brilliant and intellectually sharp blogs. Over time our interactions grew and before I knew it, we were publishing articles together. I feel blessed and proud to have been able to work with the author on a few articles that we've published together. Often we would get into intellectual discussions and I've debated and participated in many intellectual discussions during the course of my thirty-year academic journey but I've yet to find a person as perceptual, intellectually sharp, bold, and brilliant as the author of this beautifully written booklet. Apart from this booklet, the author has written on many intellectual domains, ranging from quantum mechanics to cosmology to neurosciences, and has been a source of inspiration to many of us including myself. Often while conversing with the author, I would mention that one day he will revolutionize our understanding of reality. Given the level of understanding and perception, he withholds I'm certain of it. This booklet will walk you through some of the baffling yet interesting concepts in science. In the end matter of this booklet, the author has mentioned his thoughts on different walks of existence, which will surely evoke the curiosity of a reader and will take a reader on diverse intellectual adventures.

Preface

This book contains my scientific brain droppings, concepts I've often wondered about over the past few years. As I project my mind's eye to this vast infinitude and bottomless ocean of existence, I'm struck by wonder and engulfed by awe. This book gives a glimpse of the great cosmic saga our cosmos has gone through—explaining briefly some baffling concepts that dwell in the realm of modern science. I've always been interested in the cosmic unknowns and cosmic mysteries. This book is a reflection of my interests. Although written in a technical language, if you manage to survive the technicality of this book, I submit to you, the cosmos will be yours.

The end matter contains brief notes which capture my thoughts that often knock the door of my mind after reflecting on different scientific concepts. Mostly these thoughts are grounded in established science and are arrived at via the method of deduction.

CHAPTER ONE

The Universe

A Thought

What if all our knowledge that we've managed to acquire, as species, is true only in the domain of linear-causality; this perfect notion that A causes B causes C, where everything has a straight forward and linear cause. But what about nonlinear causality? Leading theories of physics and cosmology are already surrounded by non linear causality! From Code theoretic axiom to self simulation hypothesis, everything seems to point to the existence of non linear causality. Mathematics has beautifully demonstrated the concept of nonlinear causality, like, retro-causality, in Einstein's "Block Universe" where all time exists all the time, in other words, what we call past, present and future co-exist simultaneously in this active feedback loop, wherein past effects the future but also future equally effects the past in a feedback loop. Consider our fundamental notion of universe, like second law of thermodynamics or the arrow of time, they all exhibit the characteristics of linear causality but what if all of our laws and theories are simply anthropomorphic in a sense that they're true only in the realm of human logic and linear causality. What if the actual laws governing the flow of existence do not operate in linear causality? What if they're nonlinear in their interactional landscape thereby incomprehensible for human intellect. We may be the delusional and hubristic in thinking that we've figured out the laws governing the cosmos.

To The Universe

The best-supported theory of our universe's origin centers on an event known as the big bang. This theory was born of the observation that other galaxies are moving away from our own at great speed in all directions, as if they had all been propelled by an ancient explosive force. A Belgian priest named Georges Lemaître first suggested the big bang theory in the 1920s, when he theorized that the universe began from a single primordial atom. The idea received major boosts from Edwin Hubble's observations that galaxies are speeding away from us in all directions, as well as from the 1960s discovery of cosmic microwave radiation — interpreted as echoes of the big bang — by Arno Penzias and Robert Wilson. Further work has helped clarify the big bang's tempo. Here's the theory: In the first 10^{-43} seconds of its existence, the universe was very compact, less than a million billion billionth the size of a single atom. It's thought that at such an incomprehensibly dense, energetic state, the four fundamental forces — gravity, electromagnetism, and the strong and weak nuclear forces — were forged into a single force, but our current theories haven't yet figured out how a single, unified force would work. To pull this off, we'd need to know how gravity works on the subatomic scale, but we currently don't. It's also thought that the extremely close quarters allowed the universe's very first particles to mix, mingle, and settle into roughly the same temperature. Then, in an unimaginably small fraction of a second, all that matter and energy expanded outward more or less evenly, with tiny variations provided by fluctuations on the quantum scale. That model of breakneck expansion, called inflation, may explain why the universe has such an even temperature and distribution of matter. After inflation, the universe continued to expand but at a much slower rate. It's still unclear what exactly powered inflation.

Aftermath of cosmic inflation

As time passed and matter cooled, more diverse kinds of particles began to form, and they eventually condensed into the stars and galaxies of our present universe. By the time the universe was a billionth of a second old, the universe had cooled down enough for the four fundamental forces to separate from one another. The universe's fundamental particles also formed. It was still so hot, though, that these particles hadn't yet assembled into many of the subatomic particles we have today, such as the proton. As the universe kept expanding, this piping-hot primordial soup — called the quarkgluon plasma — continued to cool. Some particle colliders, such as

CERN's Large Hadron Collider, are powerful enough to re-create the quark-gluon plasma. Radiation in the early universe was so intense that colliding photons could form pairs of particles made of matter and antimatter, which is like regular matter in every way except with the opposite electrical charge. It's thought that the early universe contained equal amounts of matter and antimatter. But as the universe cooled, photons no longer packed enough punch to make matter-antimatter pairs. So like an extreme game of musical chairs, many particles of matter and antimatter paired off and annihilated one another. Somehow, some excess matter survived — and it's now the stuff that people, planets, and galaxies are made of. Our existence is a clear sign that the laws of nature treat matter and antimatter slightly differently. Researchers have experimentally observed this rule imbalance, called CP violation, in action. Physicists are still trying to figure out exactly how matter won out in the early universe.

Building atoms

Within the universe's first second, it was cool enough for the remaining matter to coalesce into protons and neutrons, the familiar particles that make up atoms' nuclei. And after the first three minutes, the protons and neutrons had assembled into hydrogen and helium nuclei. By mass, hydrogen was 75 percent of the early universe's matter, and helium was 25 percent. The abundance of helium is a key prediction of big bang theory, and it's been confirmed by scientific observations. Despite having atomic nuclei, the young universe was still too hot for electrons to settle in around them to form stable atoms. The universe's matter remained an electrically charged fog that was so dense, light had a hard time bouncing its way through. It would take another 380,000 years or so for the universe to cool down enough for neutral atoms to form — a pivotal moment called recombination. The cooler universe made it transparent for the first time, which let the photons rattling around within it finally zip through unimpeded. We still see this primordial afterglow today as cosmic microwave background radiation, which is found throughout the universe. The radiation is similar to that used to transmit TV signals via antennae. But it is the oldest radiation known and may hold many secrets about the universe's earliest moments.

From the first stars to today

There wasn't a single star in the universe until about 180 million years after the big bang. It took that long for gravity to gather clouds of hydrogen and forge them into stars. Many physicists think that vast clouds of dark matter, a still-unknown material that outweighs visible matter by more than five to one, provided a gravitational scaffold for the first galaxies and stars. Once the universe's first stars ignited, the light they unleashed packed enough punch to once again strip electrons from neutral atoms, a key chapter of the universe called reionization. In February 2018, an Australian team announced that they may have detected signs of this "cosmic dawn." By 400 million years after the big bang, the first galaxies were born. In the billions of years since, stars, galaxies, and clusters of galaxies have formed and re-formed — eventually yielding our home galaxy, the Milky Way, and our cosmic home, the solar system. Even now the universe is expanding, and to astronomers' surprise, the pace of expansion is accelerating. It's thought that this acceleration is driven by a force that repels gravity called dark energy. We still don't know what dark energy is, but it's thought that it makes up 68 percent of the universe's total matter and energy. Dark matter makes up another 27 percent. In essence, all the matter you've ever seen — from your first love to the stars overhead — makes up less than five percent of the universe.

CHAPTER TWO

What Does It All Mean

A Thought (God & Feelings)

The endless cycles of pain and happiness that dwell the realm of life, life seems to be dictated by the laws that do not reconcile the phenomenon of feelings and pain in their formulations yet the conscious sub-systems of reality, such as humans exhibit the curse of feelings. I've long thought about the emergence of feelings in the landscape of life and I don't see any justifiable explanation for their emergence. Offcourse, I may be looking in an anthropomorphic sense and thereby making the questions obsolete in any objective sense. When I reflect on the subjective aspects of life the feeling and emotions, the turmoil and even joyfulness they bring about on the systems exhibiting them I'm forced to conclude that life would have been better without these subjective aspects. Of course, our feelings & emotions do exhibit the evolutionary advantage and actually help us to navigate the landscape of life but because of these subjectiveaspects the element of pain the dwells the realm of existence highlights itself in the conscious landscape. Sometimes thinking about emotions and subjective feeling I've often wondered about the possibility of intelligent design of the universe. Not that I actually believe in it but may be that's the basis of theology and the concept of God. May be the emotional and feeling aspects of our being actually drives the concept of God. Our intrinsic need to make sense of everything and attribute patterns to Intentional design might be the origin of the concept of God. Not only that but we're systems with conscious and emotional aspect that makes us to look for anthropomorphic explanations even when there are none. Because a conscious system is experiencing the emotions and feelings and actually going through the fuss of subjectivity, it makes sense why any conscious system would look for explanations for everything they go through - thinking that what they feel has some cosmic significance and thereby happens for some reason and must have some explanation. This is where the concept of God might arise from, the desperation for explanations and the assumption of an intentional causality. Also, I wonder if God is the natural derivative of the amount of brain computation that we withold. What do I mean by that, take an example of any other species on earth, they don't seem to be bothered by the concept of God and as far as I know there are no religious groups in animal kingdom other than humans, like, I have not met any Christian chimp or a Hindu lion yet. May be the notion of God is the natural and intrensic characteristic of the amount of computation that human brain witholds, which on the computational landscape makes it a beautiful phenomenon. The notion of God although non scientific does reflect the emance computational power we withold as species.

What Does It All Mean

In our never-ending quest for meaning, efforts to understand the Cosmos and our connection to it have been going on since time immemorial. But when confronted with a clear night sky, most people are understandably overwhelmed. Our distant ancestors were likely even frightened by what they saw. Yet aside from the few who still think that our Earth is flat, on some level everyone knows that we live on a spherical planet, circling a massive ball of thermonuclear fusion. And that we live in a sea of such stars; billions of which are bound by gravity into an agglomeration we call a galaxy. But that's usually about as much as most people understand. It's taken thousands of years to get to our present level of astronomical knowledge. Only a hundred years ago at Lowell Observatory in Arizona and later at Mount Palomar Observatory in California, astronomers realized that the universe was expanding and that our galaxy was just one among many. Today, we know there are hundreds of billions of such galaxies that stretch across cosmic time. ut today, despite great progress in cosmology and theoretical physics, there's arguably a reluctance among the scientific community to openly discuss any meaning they can glean from the universe. Too often they relegate this to religion. However, religion is really not equipped to invoke meaning from science. In journalism, the basic tenets of reporting are who, what, where and when. But arguably, the most important is why? And why is a question that astronomers and cosmologists are usually not well-equipped to answer. Often, leading theorists dismiss the universe as being the way it is, just because that's how it is. The late Nobel laureate and theoretical physicist Steven Weinberg famously wrote more than three decades ago that "The more the universe seems comprehensible, the more it also seems pointless." Weinberg, recognized as the principal architect of the standard model of particle physics, also asserted that we'll never know why the laws of nature are as they are; noting that a mystery will always remain. But we are curious creatures living in bizarre times, an era in which strains due to this pandemic as well as the stressors of geopolitics, climate change and the culture wars are exposing the extremely frayed fabric of society at large. Thus, it's only natural to take solace under a calm, clear night sky and to question all there is and all there will ever be. What's wrong with attempting to wring philosophical meaning from 2000 years of astronomical observations? We remain a bit hamstrung since our understanding of cosmology is still in its infancy. We can't prove that there are other universes; we can't prove that we live in a cosmic bubble that may be one of many that make up a multiverse. We can only scientifically prove that the universe is expanding and originated from a finite beginning, likely from a random quantum fluctuation. We still don't understand the asymmetry of time —- why it only flows in one direction. We still can't account for the ultimate composition of dark matter and dark energy which in total make up some 95 percent of the of the observable Universe. And we still don't fully understand how the Universe's fundamental forces and the laws of physics as we know them came about. As we lurch towards the mid-21st century, I can sympathize with researchers who are wary of being drawn into theological and cultural debates over the current state of cosmology. Even so, it would be great if the cosmological community at large would spend more time looking for the deeper meaning of the Cosmos as we understand it. Our own mortality; our link to the Cosmos beyond our own atmosphere; and the hunt for other life in the Universe. These are issues that weigh on each of us, even if unconsciously. Thus, it would be nice if the world's astrophysics community would make just a bit more effort to place our current cosmological knowledge in a philosophical context. As the late theoretical physicist Stephen Hawking put it, "Look up at the stars and not down at your feet. Try to make sense of what you see, and wonder about what makes the universe exist. Be curious." For we are the cosmic wonderers destained to sail the ship of this bottemless ocean of existence.

CHAPTER THREE

The Anthropic Principle

A thought

Contrary to the popular mirage of social, psychological, physical, emotional, or economic hierarchies, we all dwell in the same delusional bubbles. Imagine a colony of worms living inside a tiny mud pit on the shore of a river. This colony has rules, norms, laws, and social structure, let's assume it does! - and all of which are based on the notion of survival of this colony. The individuals of this colony may do some, apparently, voluntary movements, claiming the power of free will & choice. But we know all their actions are fully deterministic. Such a colony of worms is homomorphic to us human beings. As species, we also live our lives in a survival-centric interface, built upon the axioms of fitness payoffs, dictated & directed by laws of evolution and natural selection. Like that colony of worms, the complex computation of our brains creates the Mirage of free will and choice when in reality all of our actions are entirely governed by laws of causality and evolution. We all share the same universe, the same laws of nature, and the same fundamental task of creating, subjective, survival centric, meaning and of mattering for ourselves and those around us in the brief amount of time we have on this third rock of the sun. Three billion heartbeats, the clock is ticking!

The Anthropic Principle

The Universe exists and we are here to observe it tells us a lot. But it doesn't tell us as much as some people infer. The Universe has the fundamental laws that we observe it to have. Also, we exist, and are made of the things we're made of, obeying those same fundamental laws. And therefore, we can construct two very simple statements that would be very difficult to argue against:

1. We must be prepared to take account of the fact that our location in the Universe is necessarily privileged to the extent of being compatible with our existence as observers.

2. The Universe (and hence the fundamental parameters on which it depends) must be as to admit the creation of observers within it at some stage.

These two statements, spoken first by physicist Brandon Carter in 1973, are known, respectively, as the Weak Anthropic Principle and the Strong Anthropic Principle. They simply note that we exist within this Universe, which has the fundamental parameters, constants and laws that it has. And our existence is proof enough that the Universe allows for creatures like us to come into existence within it. A young star cluster in a star forming region, which may be giving rise to future observers right now. These simple, self-evident facts actually carry a lot of weight. It tells us that our Universe does exist with such properties that an intelligent observer could possibly have evolved within it. This stands starkly in contrast to properties that are incompatible with intelligent life, which cannot describe our Universe, on the grounds that no one would ever exist to observe it. That we are here to observe the Universe — that we actively engage in the act of observing — implies that the Universe is wired in such a way to admit our existence. This is the essence of the Anthropic Principle. It enables us to make a number of legitimate, scientific statements and predictions about the Universe as well. The fact that we are observers made of carbon tells us that the Universe must have created carbon in some fashion, and led Fred Hoyle to predict that an excited state of the carbon-12 nucleus must exist at a particular energy so that three helium-4 nuclei could fuse into carbon-12 in the interior of stars. Five years later, the discovery of both the theoretical Hoyle State and the mechanism for forming it — the triple-alpha process — was discovered and confirmed by nuclear physicist Willie Fowler, leading to an understanding of how the heavy elements in the Universe were built up in stars throughout the Universe's history.

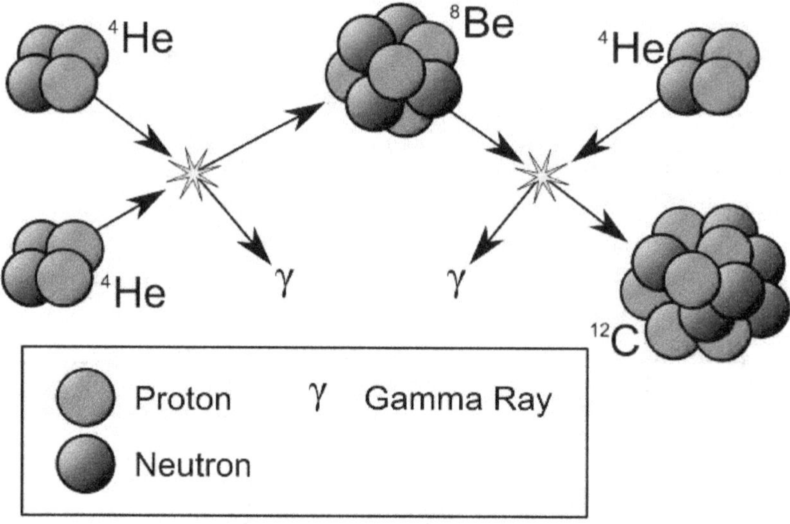

The prediction of the Hoyle State and the discovery of the triple-alpha process is perhaps the most stunningly successful use of anthropic reasoning in scientific history. Image credit: Wikimedia Commons user Borb.

Calculating what the value of our Universe's vacuum energy -- the energy inherent to empty space itself -- should be from quantum field theory gives an absurd value that's far too high. The energy of empty space determines how quickly the Universe's expansion rate grows (or its contraction rate grows, if it's negative); if it were too high, we never could have formed life, planets, stars or even molecules and atoms themselves. Given that the Universe arose with galaxies, stars, planets and human beings on it, the value of the Universe's vacuum energy, Steven Weinberg calculated in 1987, must be no higher than 10^{-118} times the number our naïve calculations give us. When we discovered dark energy in 1998, we actually measured that number for the first time, and concluded it was 10^{-120} times the naïve prediction. The anthropic principle guided us where our calculational power had failed.

Yet the original two surprisingly simple statements, the Weak and Strong

Anthropic Principles, have been misinterpreted so thoroughly that now they're routinely used to justify illogical, non-scientific statements. People claim that the anthropic principle supports a multiverse; that the anthropic principle provides evidence for the string landscape; that the anthropic principle requires we have a large gas giant to protect us from asteroids; that the anthropic principle explains why we're located at the distance we are from the galactic center. In other words, people use the anthropic principle to argue that the Universe must be exactly as it is because we exist the way we do. And that's not only untrue, it's not even what the anthropic principle says.

The anthropic principle simply says that we, observers, exist. And that we exist in this Universe, and therefore the Universe exists in a way that it allows observers to come into existence. If you set up the laws of physics so that the existence of observers is impossible, what you've set up clearly doesn't describe our Universe. The evidence for our existence means the Universe allows our existence, but it doesn't mean the Universe must have unfolded exactly this way. It doesn't mean our existence is mandatory. And it doesn't mean the Universe must have given rise to us exactly as we are. In other words, you cannot say "the Universe must be the way it is because we're here." That's not anthropics at all; that's a logical fallacy. So how did we wind up here?

In 1986, John Barrow and Frank Tipler wrote an influential book, The Anthropic Cosmological Principle, where they redefined the principles. They stated:

The observed values of all physical and cosmological quantities are not equally probably but they take on values restricted by the requirement that there exists sites where carbon-based life can evolve and by the requirement that the Universe be old enough for it to have already done so.

The Universe must have those properties which allow life to develop within it at some stage in history.

So instead of "our existence as observers means that the laws of the Universe must be such that the existence of observers is possible," we get "the Universe must allow carbon-based, intelligent life and that Universes were life doesn't develop within it are disallowed." Barrow and Tipler go further, and offer alternative interpretations, including:

The Universe, as it exists, was designed with the goal of generating and sustaining observers.

Observers are necessary to bring the Universe into being.

An ensemble of Universes with different fundamental laws and constants are necessary for our Universe to exist.

If that last one sounds a lot like a bad interpretation of the multiverse, it's because all of Barrow and Tipler's scenarios are based on bad interpretations of a self-evident principle!

It's true that we do exist in this Universe, and that the laws of nature are what they are. By looking at what unknowns might be constrained by the fact of our existence, we can learn something about our Universe. In that sense, the anthropic principle has scientific value! But if you start speculating about what the relationship between humanity, observers or other post hoc ergo propter hoc arguments, you are missing out on your opportunity to actually understand the Universe. Don't fall for bad anthropic arguments; the fact that we're here can't tell us why the Universe is this way and not any other. But if you want to better predict the parameters in the Universe we actually have, the fact that we exist can guide you to a solution you might not have arrived at by any other means.

CHAPTER FOUR

What Lies Beyond The Universe

A Thought

The second law of thermodynamics, put forth by Rudolf Clausius, says that the entropy, chaos, or disorder of the universe is continuously increasing. Ludwig Boltzmann's equation of entropy then precisely calculates the entropy, chaos, or disorder of any system. Using these two ideas it's logical to think that the universe is headed toward the lifeless, cold, dark state of maximum disorder. That's how scientists predict that the universe will end in a "big crunch" or "Big rip" or maybe keep expanding forever into nothingness. But this approach neglects something very important. I think the universe is going in a completely opposite direction, i.e, not toward the state of maximum disorder but towards the state of maximum organized complexity. For instance, take an example of life, If you think of the universe as one year old then life arose just a day ago, that's how recent the phenomenon of life is. But according to the law of entropy, the universe started in the highest possible ordered state & has been moving towards disorder & chaos ever since. If that is true, where did the organized systems of the universe, such as life, arise from? And not just simple systems but highly organized, complex, intelligent, and conscious systems. So what's going on here? Well, I think Universe is not getting random & random, it's getting more & more complex, in the organization of its subsystems & all the complex organized phenomena such as life, the human brain, consciousness, etc. are the manifestations of that increasingly complexity. This makes it plausible that the universe might be evolving towards one coherent, complex, organized system, homomorphic to a brain consisting of billions of subsystems that integrate together to form one giant system which generates and processes information collectively to, possibly, give rise to some sort of collective experience.

What Lies Beyond The Universe

It's one of the most compelling questions you could possibly ask, one that humanity has been asking since basically the beginning of time: What's beyond the known limits? What's past the edge of our maps? The ultimate version of this question is, what lies outside the boundary of the universe? The answer is ... well, it's complicated. To answer the question of what's outside the universe, we first need to define exactly what we mean by "universe." If you take it to mean literally all the things that could possibly exist in all of space and time, then there can't be anything outside the universe. Even if you imagine the universe to have some finite size, and you imagine something outside that volume, then whatever is outside also has to be included in the universe. Even if the universe is a formless, shapeless, nameless void of absolutely nothing, that's still a thing and is counted on the list of "all the things" — and, hence, is, by definition, a part of the universe. If the universe is infinite in size, you don't really need to worry about this conundrum. The universe, being all there is, is infinitely big and has no edge, so there's no outside to even talk about. Oh, sure, there's an outside to our observable patch of the universe. The cosmos is only so old, and light only travels so fast. So, in the history of the universe, we haven't received light from every single galaxy. The current width of the observable universe is about 90 billion light-years. And presumably, beyond that boundary, there's a bunch of other random stars and galaxies. The case of the curvature Cosmologists aren't sure if the universe is infinitely big or just extremely large.

To measure the universe, astronomers instead look at its curvature. The geometric curve on large scales of the universe tells us about its overall shape. If the universe is perfectly geometrically flat, then it can be infinite. If it's curved, like Earth's surface, then it has finite volume. Current observations and measurements of the curvature of the universe indicate that it is almost perfectly flat. You might think this means the universe is infinite. But it's not that simple. Even in the case of a flat universe, the cosmos doesn't have to be infinitely big. Take, for example, the surface of a cylinder. It is geometrically flat, because parallel lines drawn on the surface remain parallel (that's one of the definitions of "flatness"), and yet it has a finite size. The same could be true of the universe: It could be completely flat yet closed in on itself. But even if the universe is finite, it doesn't necessarily mean there is an edge or an outside. It could be that our three dimensional universe is embedded in some larger, multidimensional construct. That's perfectly fine and is indeed a part of some exotic models of physics. But currently, we have no way of testing that, and it doesn't really affect the day-to-day operations of the cosmos. And I know this is extremely headache-inducing, but even if the universe has a finite volume, it doesn't have to be embedded A matter of perspective When you imagine the universe, you might think of a giant ball that's filled with stars, galaxies and all sorts of interesting astrophysical objects. You may imagine how it looks from the outside, like an astronaut views the globe of the Earth from a serene orbit above. But the universe doesn't need that outside perspective in order to exist. The universe simply is. It is entirely mathematically self-consistent to define a three-dimensional universe without requiring an outside to that universe. When you imagine the universe as a ball floating in the middle of nothing, you're playing a mental trick on yourself that the mathematics does not require. Granted, it sounds impossible for there to be a finite universe that has nothing outside it. And not even "nothing" in the sense of an empty void — completely and totally mathematically undefined. In fact, asking "What's outside the universe?" is like asking "What sound does the color purple make?" It's a nonsense question, because you're trying to combine two unrelated concepts. It could very well be that our universe does indeed have an "outside." But again, this doesn"t have to be the case. There's nothing in mathematics that describes the universe that demands an outside. If all this sounds complicated and confusing, don't worry. The entire point of developing sophisticated mathematics is to have tools that give us the ability to grapple with concepts beyond what we can imagine. And that's one of the powers of modern cosmology: It allows us to study the unimaginable.

The Unknown Origins

Where did all of this come from ? The question that never stops haunting me. The more curious we get about the great cosmic unknowns, the more unanswered questions our investigations of the Universe will reveal. Inquiring about the nature of anything — where it is, where it came from, and how it came to be — will inevitably lead you to the same great mysteries:

about the ultimate nature and origin of the Universe and everything in it. Yet, no matter how far back we go, those same lingering questions always seem to remain: at some point, the entities that are our "starting point" didn't necessarily exist, so how did they come to be? Eventually, you wind up at the ultimate question: how did something arise from nothing? As many recent questioners, including Luke Martin, Buzz Morse, Russell Blalack, John Heiss and many others have written: How did something (the universe/big bang) come from nothing? This is maybe one of the biggest questions of all, because it's basically asking not only where did everything come from, but how did all of it arise in the first place. Here's as far as science has gotten us, at least, so far. Today, when we look out at the Universe, the full suite of observations we've collected, even with the known uncertainties taken into account, all point towards a remarkably consistent picture. Our Universe is made of matter (rather than antimatter), obeys the same laws of physics everywhere and at all times, and began — at least, as we know it — with a hot Big Bang some 13.8 billion years ago. It's governed by General Relativity, it's expanding and cooling and gravitating, and it's dominated by dark energy (68%) and dark matter (27%), with normal matter, neutrinos, and radiation making up the rest. Today, of course, it's full of galaxies, stars, planets, heavy elements, and in at least one location, intelligent and technologically advanced life. These structures weren't always there, but rather arose as a result of cosmic evolution. In a remarkable scientific leap, 20th century scientists were able to reconstruct the timeline for how our Universe went from a mostly uniform Universe, devoid of complex structure and consisting exclusively of hydrogen and helium, to the structure rich Universe we observe today. If we start from today, we can step backwards in time, and ask where any individual structure or component of that structure came from. For each answer we get, we can then ask, "ok, but where did that come from and how did that arise," going back until we're forced to answer, "we don't know, at least not yet." Then, at last, we can contemplate what we have, and ask, "how did that arise, and is there a way that it could have arisen from nothing?" So, let's get started. The life we have today comes from complex molecules, which must have arisen from the atoms of the periodic table: the raw ingredients that make up all the normal matter we have in the Universe today. The Universe wasn't born with these atoms; instead, they required multiple generations of stars living-and dying, with the products of their nuclear reactions recycled into future generations of stars. Without this, planets and complex chemistry would be an impossibility. In order to form modern stars and galaxies, we need: gravitation to pull small galaxies and star clusters into one another, creating large galaxies and triggering new waves of star formation, which required pre-existing collections of mass, created from gravitational growth, which require dark matter haloes to form early on, preventing star forming episodes from ejecting that matter back into the intergalactic medium, which require the right balance of normal matter, dark matter, and radiation to give rise to the cosmic microwave background, the light elements formed in the hot Big Bang, and the abundances/patterns we see in them, which required initial seed fluctuations — density imperfections — to gravitationally grow into these structures, which require some way of creating these imperfections, along with some way of creating dark matter and creating the initial amounts of normal matter. These are three key ingredients that are required, in the early stages of the hot Big Bang, to give rise to the Universe as we observe it today. Assuming that we also require the laws of physics and spacetime itself to exist — along with matter/energy itself — we probably want to include those as the necessary ingredients that must somehow arise.

So, in short, when we ask whether we can get a Universe from nothing or not, these are the novel, hitherto unexplained entities that we need to somehow arise. To get more matter than antimatter, we have to extrapolate back into the very early Universe, to a time when our physics is very much uncertain. The laws of physics as we know them are in some sense symmetric between matter and antimatter: every reaction we've ever created or observed can only create or-destroy matter and antimatter in equal amounts. But the Universe we had, despite beginning in an incredibly hot and dense state where matter and antimatter could both be created in abundant, copious amounts, must have had some way to create a matter/antimatter asymmetry where none existed initially. There are many ways to accomplish this. Although we don't know which scenario actually took place in our young Universe, all ways of doing so involve the following three elements:

1. an out-of-equilibrium set of conditions, which naturally arise in an expanding, cooling Universe,

2. a way to generate baryon-number-violating interactions, which the Standard Model allows through sphaleron interactions (and beyond-the-Standard-Model scenarios allow in additional ways),

3. and a way to generate enough C and CP violation to create a matter/

antimattery asymmetry in great enough amounts. The Standard Model has all of these ingredients, but not enough.

If you consider a matter/antimatter symmetric Universe as "a Universe with nothing," then it's almost guaranteed that the Universe generated something from nothing, even though we aren't quite certain exactly how it happened.

Similarly, there are lots of viable ways to generate dark matter. We know — from extensive testing and searching — that whatever dark matter is, it can't be composed of any particles that are present in the Standard Model. Whatever its true nature is, it requires new physics beyond what's presently known. But there are many ways it could have been created, including: • from being thermally created in the hot, early Universe, and then failing to completely annihilate away, remaining stable thereafter (like the lightest supersymmetric or Kaluza Klein particle), • or from a phase transition that spontaneously occurred as the Universe expanded and cooled, ripping massive particles out of the quantum vacuum (e.g., the axion), • as a new form of a neutrino, which itself can either mix with the known neutrinos (i.e., a sterile neutrino), or as a heavy right-handed neutrino that exists in addition to the conventional neutrinos, • or as a purely gravitational phenomenon that gives rise to an ultramassive particle (e.g., a WIMPzilla). Why is there dark matter, today, when the remainder of the Universe appears to work just fine early on without it? There must have been some way to generate this "thing" where there wasn't such a thing beforehand, but all of these scenarios require energy. So, then, where did all that energy come from? Perhaps, according to cosmic inflation — our leading theory of the Universe's pre-Big Bang origins — it really did come from nothing. This requires a little bit of an explanation, and is what is most frequently meant by "a Universe from nothing."

When you imagine the earliest stages of the hot Big Bang, you have to think of something incredibly hot, dense, high-energy, and almost perfectly uniform. When we ask, "how did this arise," we typically have two options.

1. We can go the Lady Gaga route, and just claim it must've been "born this way." The Universe was born with these properties, which we call initial conditions, and there's no further explanation. As a student of science, I call this approach "giving up."

2. Or we can do what scientists do best: try and concoct a theoretical mechanism that could explain the initial conditions, teasing out concrete predictions that differ from the standard, prevailing theory's predictions

and then going out seeking to measure the critical parameters.

Cosmic inflation came about as a result of taking that second approach, and it literally changed our conception of how our Universe came to be. Instead of extrapolating "hot and dense" back to an infinitely hot, infinitely dense singularity, inflation basically says, "perhaps the hot Big Bang was preceded by a period where an extremely large energy density was present in the fabric of space itself, causing the Universe to expand at a relentless (inflationary) rate, and then when inflation ended, that energy got transferred into matter-and-antimatter-and radiation, creating what we see as the hot Big Bang: the aftermath of inflation." In gory detail, this not only creates a Universe with the same temperature everywhere, spatial flatness, and no leftover relics from a hypothetical grand unified epoch, but also predicts a particular type and spectrum of seed (density) fluctuations, which we then went out and saw. From just empty space itself — although it is empty space filled with a large amount of field energy — a natural process has created the entire observable Universe, rich in structure, as we see it today. That's the big idea of getting a Universe from nothing, but it isn't satisfying to everyone. To a large fraction of people, a Universe where space-and time still exist, along with the laws of physics, the fundamental constants, and some non-zero field energy inherent to the fabric of space itself, is very much divorced from the idea of nothingness. We can imagine, after all, a location outside of space; a moment beyond the confines of time; a set of conditions that have no physical reality to constrain them. And those imaginings — if we define these physical realities as things we need to eliminate to obtain true nothingness — are certainly valid, at least philosophically. But that's the difference between philosophical nothingness and a more physical definition of nothingness. As we know now, there are four scientific definitions of nothing, and they're all valid, depending on your context:

1. A time when your "thing" of interest didn't exist,

2. Empty, physical space,

3. Empty spacetime in the lowest-energy state possible, and

4. Whatever you're left with when you take away the entire Universe and the laws governing it.

We can definitely say we obtained "a Universe from nothing" if we use the first two definitions; we cannot if we use the third; and quite unfortunately, we don't know enough to say what happens if we use the fourth. Without a physical theory to describe what happens outside of the Universe and beyond the realm physical laws, the concept of true nothingness is physically ill-defined. In the context of physics, it's impossible to make sense of an idea of absolute nothingness. What does it mean to be outside of space and time, and how can space and time sensibly, predictably emerge from a state of non-existence? How can spacetime emerge at a particular location or time, when there's no definition of location or time without it? Where do the rules governing quanta — the fields and particles both — arise from? This line of thought even assumes that space, time, and the laws of physics themselves weren't eternal, when in fact they may be. Any theorems or proofs to the contrary rely on assumptions whose validity is not soundly established under the conditions which we'd seek to apply them. If you accept a physical definition of "nothing," then yes, the Universe as we know it very much appears to have arisen from nothing. But if you leave physical constraints behind, then all certainly about our ultimate cosmic origins disappears. Unfortunately for us all, inflation, by its very nature, erases any information that might be imprinted from a pre-existing state on our observable Universe. Despite the limitless nature of our imaginations, we can only draw conclusions about matters for which tests involving our physical reality can be constructed. No matter how logically sound any other consideration may be, including a notion of absolute nothingness, it's merely a construct of our minds.

CHAPTER FIVE

The Multiverse

Do we really live in a multiverse, or is this notion beyond the pale of science? Multiverse ideas have traditionally received short shrift from the establishment: Giordano Bruno with his infinite space multiverse got burned at the stake in 1600 and Hugh Everett with his quantum multiverse got burned on the physics job market in 1957. There's been a sea-change in recent years, however. Parallel universes are now all the rage, cropping up in books, movies and even jokes: "You passed your exam in many parallel universes — but not this one." This airing of ideas certainly hasn't led to a consensus among scientists, but it's made the multiverse debate much more nuanced and, in my opinion, more interesting, with scientists moving beyond shouting sound bites past each other and genuinely trying to understand opposing points of view. George Ellis's new article is a great example of this, and I highly recommend reading it if you haven't already. By our universe, I mean the spherical region of space from which light has had time to reach us during the 13.7 billion years since our big bang. When talking about parallel universes, I find it useful to use Max Tegmark's classification of multiverse, of four different levels:

Level I (other such regions far away in space where the apparent laws of physics are the same, but where history played out differently because things started out differently),

Level II (regions of space where even the apparent laws of physics are different),

Level III(parallel worlds elsewhere in the so-called Hilbert space where quantum reality plays out), and Level IV (totally disconnected realities governed by different mathematical equations). In his critique, George Ellis classifies many of the arguments in favor of these multiverse levels and argues that they all have problems. Here's my summary of his main anti-multiverse arguments:

1) Inflation may be wrong (or not eternal)

2) Quantum mechanics may be wrong (or not unitary)

3) String theory may be wrong (or lack multiple solutions)

4) Multiverses may be unfalsifiable

5) Some claimed multiverse evidence is dubious

6) Fine-tuning arguments may assume too much

7) It's a slippery slope to even bigger multiverses (George Ellis didn't actually mention (2) in the article, but I'm adding it here because I think he would have if the editor had allowed him more than six pages.) What's my take on this critique? Interestingly, I agree with all of these seven statements — and nonetheless, I'll still happily bet my life savings on the existence of a multiverse! Let's start with the first four. Inflation naturally produces the Level I multiverse, and if you add in string theory with a landscape of possible solutions, you get Level II, too. Quantum mechanics in its mathematically simplest ("unitary") form gives you Level III. So if these theories are ruled out, then key evidence for these multiverses collapses. Remember: Parallel universes are not a theory — they are predictions of certain theories. To me, the key point is that if theories are scientific, then it's legitimate science to work out and discuss all their consequences even if they involve unobservable entities. For a theory to be falsifiable, we need not be able to observe and test all its predictions, merely at least one of them. My answer to (4) is therefore that what's scientifically testable are our mathematical theories, not necessarily their implications, and that this is quite OK. For example, because Einstein's theory of general relativity has successfully predicted many things that we can observe, we also take seriously its predictions for things we cannot observe, e.g., what happens inside black holes. Likewise, if we're impressed by the successful predictions of inflation or quantum mechanics so far, then we need to take seriously also their other predictions, including the Level I and Level III multiverse. George Ellis even mentions the possibility that eternal inflation may one day be ruled out — to me, this is simply an argument that eternal inflation is a scientific theory. String theory certainly hasn't come as far as inflation and quantum mechanics in terms of establishing itself as a testable scientific theory. However, I suspect that we'll be stuck with a Level II multiverse even if string theory turns out to be a red herring. It's quite common for mathematical equations to have multiple solutions, and as long as the fundamental equations describing our reality do, then eternal inflation generically creates huge regions of space that physically realize

each of these solutions.

For example, the equations governing water molecules, which have nothing to do with string theory, permit the three solutions corresponding to steam, liquid water and ice, and if space itself can similarly exist in different phases, inflation will tend to realize them all. George Ellis lists a number of observations purportedly supporting multiverse theories that are dubious at best, like evidence that certain constants of nature aren't really constant, evidence in the cosmic microwave background radiation of collisions with other universes or strangely connected space, etc. I totally share his skepticism to these claims. In all these cases, however, the controversies have been about the analysis of the data, much like in the cold fusion debacle. To me, the very fact that scientists are making these measurements and arguing about data details is further evidence that this is within the pale of science: this is precisely what separates a scientific controversy from a nonscientific one! Our universe appears surprisingly fine-tuned for life in the sense that if you tweaked many of our constants of nature by just a tiny amount, life as we know it would be impossible. Why? If there's a Level II multiverse where these "constants" take all possible values, it's not surprising that we find ourselves in one of the rare universes that are inhabitable, just like it's not surprising that we find ourselves living on Earth rather than Mercury or Neptune. George objects to the fact that you need to assume a multiverse theory to draw this conclusion, but that's how we test any scientific theory: we assume that it's true, work out the consequences, and discard the theory if the predictions fail to match the observations. Some of the fine-tuning appears extreme enough to be quite embarrassing — for example, we need to tune the dark energy to about 123 decimal places to make habitable galaxies. To me, an unexplained coincidence can be a tell-tale sign of a gap in our scientific understanding. Dismissing it by saying "We just got lucky — now stop looking for an explanation!" is not only unsatisfactory, but is also tantamount to ignoring a potentially crucial clue. George Ellis argues that if we take seriously that anything that could happen does happen, we're led down a slippery slope toward even larger multiverses, like the Level IV one. Since this is my favorite multiverse level, and , this is a slope that I'm happy to slide down! George Ellis also mentions that multiverses may fall foul of Occam's razor by introducing unnecessary complications. As a student of science, I judge the elegance and simplicity of a theory not by its ontology, but by the elegance and simplicity of its mathematical equations — and it's quite striking to me that the mathematically simplest theories tend to give us multiverses. It's proven remarkably hard to write down a theory which produces exactly the universe we see and nothing more. Finally, there's an anti-multiverse argument which I commend George Ellis for avoiding, but which is in my opinion the most persuasive one of all for most people: the parallel universes just seems too weird to be true. Having looked at anti-multiverse arguments, let's now analyze the pro-multiverse case a bit more closely. I'm going to argue that all the controversial issues melt away if we accept the External Reality Hypothesis: there exists an external physical reality completely independent of us humans. Suppose that this hypothesis is correct. Then most multiverse critique rests on some combination of the following three dubious assumptions:

1) Omnivision assumption: physical reality must be such that at least one observer can in principle observe all of it.

2) Pedagogical reality assumption: physical reality must be such that all reasonably informed human observers feel they intuitively understand it.

3) No-copy assumption: no physical process can copy observers or create subjectively indistinguishable observers.

(1) and (2) appear to be motivated by little more than human hubris. The omnivision assumption effectively redefines the word "exists" to be synonymous with what is observable to us humans, akin to an ostrich with its head in the sand. Those who insist on the pedagogical reality assumption will typically have rejected comfortingly familiar childhood notions like Aladin's Magic lump, local realism, the Tooth Fairy, and ghosts— but have they really worked hard enough to free themselves from comfortingly familiar notions that are more deeply rooted? In my personal opinion, our job is to try to figure out how the world works, not to tell it how to work based on our philosophical preconceptions. If the omnivision assumption is false, then there are unobservable things that exist and we live in a multiverse. If the pedagogical reality assumption is false, then the objection that multiverses are too weird makes no logical sense. If the no-copy assumption is false, then there's no fundamental reason why there can't be copies of you elsewhere in the external reality — indeed, both eternal inflation and unitary quantum mechanics provide mechanisms for creating them. We humans have a well-documented tendency toward hubris, arrogantly imagining ourselves at center stage, with everything revolving around us. We've gradually learned that it's instead we who are revolving around the sun, which is itself revolving around one galaxy among countless

others. Thanks to breakthroughs in physics, we may be gaining still deeper insights into the very nature of reality.

The price we have to pay is becoming more humble — which will probably do us good — but in return we may find ourselves inhabiting a reality grander than our ancestors dreamed of in their wildest dreams.

CHAPTER SIX

Time

Time is all around us, a constant that keeps the world and universe ticking and trying to understand it, is one of the things that keeps me awake at night. If the question "What is time?" doesn't completely mystify & bemuse you then you haven't understood the question yet. From Isaac Newton to Albert Einstein & to the baffling insights of Carlo Rovelli & Wheeler-Dewitt equation time has emerged as one of the baffling concepts of modern physics. In this chapter, I will walk you through the concept of time from Newton's "Absolute time" to timelessness of quantum mechanics. When considering time, it's easy to quickly get lost in the complexity of the topic. Time is all around us — it's ever present and is the basis of how we record life on Earth. It's the constant that keeps the world, the solar system and even the universe ticking. Civilizations have risen and fallen, stars have been born and extinguished, and our one method of keeping track of every event in the universe and on Earth has been comparing them to the present day with the regular passing of time. But is it really a constant? Is time really as simple as a movement from one second to the next? 13.8 billion years ago the universe was born, and since then time has flown by to the present day, overseeing the creation of galaxies and the expansion of space. But when it comes to comparing time, it's daunting to realize just how little of time we've actually experienced. Earth might be 4.5 billion years old, but modern humans have inhabited it for around 300,000 years — that's just 0.002% the age of the universe. Feeling small and insignificant yet? It gets worse. We've experienced so little time on Earth that in astronomical terms we're entirely negligible. In the 17th century physicist Isaac Newton saw time as an arrow fired from a bow, traveling in a direct, straight line and never deviating from its path. To Newton, one second on Earth was the same length of time as that same second on Mars, Jupiter or in deep space. He believed that absolute motion could not be detected, which meant that nothing in the universe had a constant speed, even light. By applying this theory, he was able to assume that if the speed of light could vary, then time must be constant. Time must tick from one second to the next, with no difference between the length of any two seconds. This is something that it's easy to think is true. Every day has roughly 24 hours; you don't have one day with 26 and one with 23. However, in 1905, Albert Einstein asserted that the speed of light doesn't vary, but rather it is a constant, traveling at roughly 186,282 miles per second (299,792 kilometers per second). He postulated that time was more like a river, ebbing and flowing depending on the effects of gravity and space-time. Time would speed up and slow down around cosmological bodies with differing masses and velocities, and therefore one second on Earth was not the same length of time everywhere in the universe. This posed a problem. If the speed of light was really a constant, then there had to be some variable that altered over large distances across the universe. With the universe expanding and planets and galaxies moving on a galactically humongous scale, something had to give to allow for these small fluctuations. And this variable had to be time. It was ultimately Einstein's theory that was not only believed to be the truth, but also proven to be entirely accurate. In October 1971, two physicists named J.C. Hafele and Richard Keating set about proving its validity. To do this they flew four caesium atomic clocks on planes around the world, eastwards and then westwards. According to Einstein's theory, when compared with ground based atomic clocks — in this instance at the U.S. Naval Observatory in Washington, D.C. — Hafele and Keating's airborne clocks would be about 40 nanoseconds slower after their eastward trip, and about 275 nanoseconds faster after travelling west, due to the gravitational effects of the Earth on the velocity of the planes, according to their 1972 study in the journal Science. Incredibly, the clocks did indeed register a difference when traveling east and west around the world — about 59 nanoseconds slower and 273 nanoseconds faster respectively when compared to the U.S. Naval Observatory. This proved that Einstein was correct, specifically with his theory of time dilation, and that time did indeed fluctuate throughout the universe.

What happens during time dilation?
What does the theory of special relativity mean in terms of time? I'd suggest fallowing the entire series of this topic, which won't be more than 4 articles) to truly get a grasp of time dilation. Newton and Einstein did agree on

one thing, though — that time moves forward. So far there's no evidence of anything in the universe that is able to dodge time and move forwards and backwards at will. Everything ultimately moves forward in time, be it at a regular pace or slightly warped if approaching the speed of light. Can we answer why time ticks forward, though? Not quite, although there are several theories as to why it does. One of these brings in the laws of thermodynamics, specifically the second law. This states that everything in the universe wants to move from low to high entropy, or from uniformity to disorder, beginning with simplicity at the Big Bang and moving to the almost random arrangement of galaxies and their inhabitants in the present day. This is known as the "arrow of time," or sometimes "time's arrow, likely coined by British astronomer Arthur Eddington in 1928, analytic philosopher Huw Price. Eddington suggested that time was not symmetrical: "If as we follow the arrow we find more and more of the random element in the state of the world, then the arrow is pointing towards the future; if the random element decreases, the arrow points towards the past," he wrote in "The Nature of the Physical World" in 1928. For example, if you were to observe a star in almost uniformity, but later saw it explode as a supernova and become a scattered nebula, you would know that time had moved forward from equality to chaos. Another theory suggests that the passage of time is due to the expansion of the universe. As the universe expands it pulls time with it, as space and time are linked as one, but this would mean that if the universe were to reach a theoretical limit of expansion and begin to contract, then time would reverse — a slight paradox for scientists and astronomers. Would time really move backwards, with everything coming back to an era of simplicity and ending with a "Big Crunch"? It's unlikely we'll be around to find out, but we can postulate on what we think might happen. It's incredible to think of the progress we've made in our understanding of time over the past century. From ancient time telling sundials to modern atomic clocks, we can even track the passing of a second more closely than ever before. Time remains a complex topic, but thanks to scientific visionaries, we are getting closer to unlocking the secrets of this not-so constant universal constant.

The importance of Einstein's theory of special relativity

Einstein's theory of special relativity relies on one key fact: the speed of light is the same no matter how you look at it. To put this into practice, imagine you are traveling in a car at 32km/h, and you drive past a friend who is standing still. As you pass them, you throw a ball out in front of the car at 16 km/h. To your friend the ball's speed combines with that of the car, and so appears to be travelling at 32km/h +16km/h= 48 km/h. Relative to you, however, the ball travels at only 16 km/h, as you are already travelling at 32km/h. Now imagine the same scenario, but this time you pass your stationary friend while traveling at half the speed of light. Through some imaginary contraption, your friend can observe you as you travel past. This time you shine a beam of light out of the car windscreen. In our previous calculation we added together the speed of the ball and the car to find out what your friend saw, so in this instance, does your friend see the beam of light traveling at one-and-a-half times the speed of light? According to Einstein, the answer is no. The speed of light always remains constant, and nothing can travel faster than it. On this occasion, both you and your friend observe the speed of light traveling at its universally agreed value at roughly 186,282 miles per second. This is the theory of special relativity, and it's very important when talking about time. Time: The fourth dimension of the universe It was once thought that space and time were separate, and that the universe was merely an assortment of cosmic bodies arranged in three dimensions. Einstein, however, introduced the concept of a fourth dimension — time — that meant that space and time were inextricably linked. The general theory of relativity suggests that space-time expands and contracts depending on the momentum and mass of nearby matter. The theory was sound, but all that was needed was proof. That proof came courtesy of NASA's Gravity Probe B, which demonstrated that space and time were indeed linked. Four gyroscopes were pointed in the direction of a distant star, and if gravity did not have an effect on space and time, they would remain locked in the same position. However, scientists clearly observed a "frame-dragging" effect due to the gravity of Earth, which meant the gyroscopes were pulled very slightly out of position. This seems to prove that the fabric of space itself can be altered, and if space and time are linked, then time itself can be stretched and contracted by gravity.

How long is a second?

There are two main ways of measuring time: dynamic and atomic time. The former relies on the motion of celestial bodies, including Earth, to keep track of time, whether it's the rotation time of a distant spinning star such as a pulsar, the motion of a star across our night sky or the rotation of Earth. However, a spinning star not withstanding, which can be hard to observe, these methods are not always entirely accurate. The old definition of a second was based on the rotation of Earth. As it takes the sun one day to rise in the east, set in the west and rise again, a day was almost arbitrarily divided into 24 hours, an hour into 60 minutes and a minute into 60 seconds. However, Earth doesn't rotate uniformly. Its rotation decreases at a rate of about 30 seconds every 10,000 years due to factors such as tidal friction. Scientists have devised ways to account for the changing speed of Earth's rotation, introducing leap seconds," but for the most accurate time you have to go even smaller. Atomic time relies on the energy transition within an atom of a certain element, commonly caesium. By defining a second using the number of these transitions, time can be measured with an accuracy of losing a tiny portion of a second in a million years. The definition of a second is now defined as 9,192,631,770 transitions within a caesium atom.

Atomic clocks: The most accurate track of time

The most accurate clock in the universe would probably be a rotating star like a pulsar, but on Earth atomic clocks provide the most accurate track of time. The entire GPS system in orbit around Earth uses atomic clocks to accurately track positions and relay data to the planet, while entire scientific centers are set up to calculate the most accurate measure of time — usually by measuring transitions within a caesium atom. While most atomic clocks rely on magnetic fields, modern clocks are using lasers to track and detect energy transitions within caesium atoms and keep a more definite measure of time. Although caesium clocks are currently used to keep time around the world, strontium clocks promise twice as much accuracy, while an experimental design based on charged mercury atoms could reduce discrepancies even further to less than 1 second lost or gained in 400 million years.

CHAPTER SEVEN

Dawn Of Humans On Earth

By the time our planet was four billion years old, the rise of large plants and animals was just beginning. Complexity exploded around that time, as the combination of multicellularity, sexual reproduction, and other genetic advances brought about the Cambrian explosion. Many evolutionary changes occurred over the next 500 million years, with extinction events and selection pressures paving the way for new forms of life to arise and develop. 65 million years ago, a catastrophic asteroid strike wiped out not only the dinosaurs, but practically every animal weighing over 25 kg (excepting leatherback sea turtles and some crocodiles). This was Earth's most recent great mass extinction, and it left a large number of niches unfilled in its wake. Mammals rose to prominence in the aftermath, with the first humans arising less than 1 million years ago. Here's our story. 65 million years ago, a massive asteroid somewhere between 5 and 10 kilometers in diameter struck our planet. It kicked up a layer of dust that settled all over the world, a layer that can be found today in our planet's sedimentary rock. On the older side of that layer, fossils such as dinosaurs, pterosaurs, ichthyosaurs and plesiosaurs are abundant. Giant reptiles, ammonites, and large classes of plants and animals all existed prior to that event, along with small, flying birds and the tiny, land-dwelling mammals. After that event, the mammals survived. With no larger predators to stop them, they grew, diversified, and experienced a population explosion. Primates, rodents, lagomorphs, and other forms of mammals, including placental mammals, marsupials, and even the egg-laying mammals are all abundant at the start of the Cenezoic epoch. Almost immediately, the primates began diversifying even further. 63 million years ago — just 2 million years after the demise of the dinosaurs — they split into two groups. 1. The dry-nosed primates, known formally as the haplorrhines, which developed into modern monkeys and apes.

2. The wet-nosed primates, known as the strepsirrhines, which developed into modern lemurs and aye-ayes.

58 million years ago, another big change occurred: the haplorrhines experienced an interesting genetic split, as the first novel and unique evolutionary branch became distinct from the rest of the dry-nosed primates: the tarsier. With its enormous eyes, it was uniquely well-adapted to see at night.

With its enormous eyes but a dry nose, the tarsier holds the distinction as the first haplorrhine to diverge from the mammalian lineage that would give rise to monkeys, apes, and eventually modern humans. Note that they have dry, rather than wet, noses.

The niche it now occupied was sufficiently different from the remaining groups of our ancestors that they evolved differently from the rest of their cousins from this point onwards. This type of evolutionary splitting occurs every so often, and isn't unique to primates. Although we normally don't think very much about our distant cousins and how they develop once they've split off from us, it isn't just haplorrhines like us (and our direct ancestors) that underwent interesting phases of evolution. All throughout the past 65 million years — just as it was before that time — the various mammals, birds, plants, and other living organisms evolved together. Evolution is driven by environmental changes, and that includes all the floral and faunal changes that occur on our planet. 55 million years ago, a sudden rise in greenhouse gases caused the global average temperature to swiftly rise, wiping out many deep-ocean animals and plants. This transformation left many large, unfilled niches in the ocean, paving the way for cetaceans (the large oceanic mammals) to develop. 50 million years ago, some of the even-toed mammals began evolving into sea-dwelling creatures. The artiodactyls may have all evolved from a single, common ancestor, or may have evolved independently. Animals like Indohyus, which dates to 48 million years ago, may have given rise to protocetids: shallow-water mammals that returned to land to give birth. Right around that time, 47 million years ago, the primate Darwinius masillae existed, as the fossil Ida, preserved from that time, provides a spectacular example. Although this was originally touted as a proverbial "missing link" in human evolution, Ida is not a haplorrhine like us, but a strepsirrhene: a wet-nosed primate. But another 7 million years later — 40 million years ago — an important development occurred among the dry-nosed primates: the New World monkeys branched off. Humans and our ape ancestors are descended from

Old World monkeys; New World monkeys are the first simians (or higher primates) to evolutionary diverge from our lineage. They would go on to colonize most of South America, where they are still found in abundance today.

The Old World monkeys continue to thrive and successfully occupy their niches, while diversifying in body size and physical features. 25 million years ago, the first apes evolved, splitting off from the remaining Old World monkeys at that time. The apes — defined by the complete lack of a tail of any type — would go on to give rise to many of the close relatives of humans that survive today: both the lesser apes and the great apes. The earliest ape to split off from the Old World monkeys was the Gibbon, a lesser ape that first emerged 18 million years ago. Sometime between 14 and 16 million years ago, the first great apes appeared, with Orang-utans branching off 14 million years ago. The Orang-utans spread into southern Asia after this, while the other great apes remained in Africa. The largest primate ever, Gigantopithecus, first arose some 9 million years ago, only becoming extinct a few hundred thousand years ago. 7 million years ago, gorillas branched off from the other great apes; they remain the largest of all the surviving primates. The great apes split off in two directions 6 million years ago, with one direction giving rise to humanity's ancestors and the other branch giving rise to chimpanzees and bonobos. The chimpanzee/bonobo branch remains unified for another 4 million years, with our closest surviving relatives — the chimpanzees and bonobos — diverging from one another a mere 2 million years ago. But along the track of our direct ancestors, the developments were rapid and profound. 5.6 million years ago, the first truly bipedal ape, Ardipithecus, arose. Although it's a controversial claim, the hand bones in Ardipithecus show evidence of it being a transitional fossil between the earlier great apes and the later Australopithecines. Approximately 4 million years ago, the first Australopithecus evolved: the first members of the Hominina subtribe (a taxonomic classification more specific than family but less specific than genus). Shortly thereafter, the first evidence of stone tool use appears: presently at 3.4-to-3.7 million years ago. A reproduction of Australopithecus africanus, based on the STS5 skull ("Mrs. Ples") found in Sterkfontein, South Africa, dating to 2.7 million years ago. Australopithecus was the dominant hominid throughout Africa for nearly 2 million years, until the rise of Homo habilis. (Credit: Nachosan/Wikimedia Commons) A critical evolutionary step happened a little more than 2 million years ago, as our hominid ancestors faced food shortages. One evolutionarily successful approach was to develop stronger jaws, which gave us the capability to eat foods (like nuts) that were otherwise inaccessible. But another approach was also successful: to develop weaker jaws and larger brains, enabling us to access the food. While both groups survived for a time, the larger-brained group was more adaptable to changes, and they continued to survive. This is the evolutionary path that we think led to the development of the genus Homo, which first arose about 2.5 million years ago. Homo habilis, known colloquially as "handy man," had larger brains than their Australopithecus counterparts and displayed far more widespread tool use. About 1.9 million years ago, Homo erectus evolved. This human ancestor not only walked fully upright, but had much larger brains than Homo habilis: nearly twice as large, on average. Homo erectus became the first direct human ancestor to leave Africa, and the first to display evidence of using fire. Homo habilis was likely driven to extinction more than a million years ago, as was the last Australopithecus. Across the world, new examples of the genus Homo emerged, including Homo antecessor in Europe (which may be an evolved habilis or erectus, or an early form of heidelbergensis) about 1.2 million years ago, followed by Homo heidelbergensis some 600,000 years ago. Approximately 700,000 years ago, the earliest evidence for cooking appears; about 500,000 years ago, the first evidence for clothing appears. Approximately 300,000 years ago, the first Homo sapiens — anatomically modern humans — arose alongside our other hominid relatives. It is unknown whether we descended directly from Homo erectus, heidelbergensis, or antecessor, although Neanderthals, which came slightly later at 240,000 years ago, most certainly came from Homo heidelbergensis. Modern speech is thought to have arisen almost as soon as Homo sapiens did. It took 13.8 billion years of cosmic history for the first human beings to arrive, and we did so relatively recently: just 300,000 years ago. 99.998% of the time that passed since the Big Bang had no human beings at all; our entire species has only existed for the most recent 0.002% of the Universe. Yet, in that short time, we've managed to figure out the entire cosmic story that led to our existence. Fortunately, the story won't end with us, as it's still being written. Evolutionarily speaking, human beings — or homo sapiens — have been around for a cosmic blink-of-an-eye: under half a million years. Based on how evolution works, it is unlikely there will be any humans left even just a few million years from now.

Values

The physical universe is a world without values. But meaning and purpose are the defining features of living things, they do things for good reasons (fitness payoffs centric) because there are things in the world that they value. The "meaning" and "values" are emergent phenomenon that emerges for the interactional landscape of a living system in the context of its fitness payoffs. Objectively speaking, values or meaning do not exist as the intrinsic characteristics of any system of reality. However, I wonder if they exist as objective sets of a subjective landscape; for instance, take the example of humans, could it be, as survival fitness payoffs are common across our species, likewise, is it possible that there is a well-defined homomorphism that underlies the human principals of value and assigning meaning to things, given our interface of reality exhibits a preserved structure across our species.

Ancestral Experiences

It saddens me deeply when I look back at the horrifying saga of our species. The spark of life emerged on earth billions of years ago. The vector of life driven by natural selection in its causal unfolding arrived at you and me. Our existence is not independent, we are standing on the shoulders of those that came before us. Through the written words (Books), deduction, and inference of logic (science) I've seen up close the saga of our species. Just going back 100-200 years, in our history, the horrifying face of human patheticity glares deep into my consciousness - the concept of slavery, all the horrifying wars, all these horrible existential nightmares that conscious systems went through; I was just Reading about a black slave named Peter, his picture taken, just a year or so before Abraham Lincoln on January 1, 1863, issued the Emancipation Proclamation which declared "all persons held as slaves...shell be declared free", traveled throughout the world, singing the song of horror to every soul. When I weigh the pain, turmoil, and sufferings of this existence against the joy, happiness, and peace, the former massively exceeds the latter. Your existence here is the end product of all those experiences of joy, wonder, awe, pain suffering, turmoil, and fear... that your ancestors went through. You're not just some random system, you carry with you the saga of your ancestors, they live in you and you are the manifestation of their experiences. Don't waste it, for every experience you have, always remember a very high price has been paid for it...A price you can neither comprehend nor imagine.

Life Is Not Static

Awe

The spaces of this vast cosmic sea enfold me and swallow me up like a speck. As I project my mind's eye to this bottomless ocean of existence, the insignificance of human life & its concerns glares deep into my mind, to the extent that it almost pushes me to the pit of existential nihilism. However, the fact that we can comprehend the cosmos & fathom its mysteries, at least a few of them, Kindles the light of significance & meaning inside me. It's awe-inspiring that we're part of this baffling complex recursive loop of existence, not just any part but the conscious & self-aware part of this vastness. The amazing thing is that every atom in your body came from a star that exploded. We are the end result of exploding stars. And, the atoms in your left hand probably came from a different star than your right hand. It really is the most poetic thing I know about physics: we're all stardust. We couldn't be here if stars hadn't exploded, because the elements - carbon, nitrogen, oxygen, iron, all the things that matter for evolution - weren't created at the beginning of time. They were created in the nuclear furnaces of stars. As Carl Sagan put it "The cosmos is within us. We are made of star-stuff. We are a way for the universe to know itself". People often ask me about my less interest in socializing with other people, since my childhood I seem to have developed this sense of connectivity with the cosmos which renders all other interactions obsolete. The fact that I'm a conscious system dwelling the realm of existence, capable of pondering and probing this vast cosmic sea makes me content and blissful.

A Question

As species, we evolved from the savannahs of Africa. All of our senses evolved to keep us alive, everything about us is survival-centric. In this context, it actually makes sense why we're not able to see the big picture - why things that transcend our short-term fitness payoffs feel irrelevant and insignificant. We didn't evolve to understand existence, we evolved to survive better, that's what 'natural selection' is all about. But evolution, as we know it, hasn't stopped. Our survival-centric minds are now seeking transcendence. Our intellect is evolving to transcend the short-term fitness payoffs of the animal kingdom, at least, in some of us. To be honest I find it paradoxical that a conscious system as complex as a human being fails to seek transcendence from the fitness payoffs of the animal kingdom. The people I've observed so far do not reflect, in any way or form, the capabilities that human intellect is blessed with, mostly because we're all busy chasing survival-centric short-term gains. When I ponder the realm of existence its complexity literally pushes me to intellectual agony and often an existential crisis. How people take this vast sea of existence for granted and carry on with their lives, dictated and directed by laws of evolution, is really a mystery to me.

Digital Immortality

Speaking of digital immortality that Ray Kurzweil presents a case for, in his Book titled "The singularity is near." Maybe with some advancement in companies like Neuralink, Kernel, etc. We'll have some personal version of Connectome, thereby some sort of digital imprint of mind. But I don't think "Immortality" is the word I would use for that. I understand Ray's argument but when John von Neumann coined and used the term "The singularity", it had more of an evolutionary context. Nonetheless, the question of digital immortality does open some interesting discussions. On the other hand, Immortality may be less fun than people imagine. Scarcity & finiteness seem to be essential ingredients of happiness. Then again, I may be just a mortal human desperately seeking a reason why my eventual death and the death of those I love make any sense at all.

Reality

If we don't perceive objective reality, if what we perceive is the hallucination created by the sensory inputs, which is what cutting-edge neuroscience is suggesting, then why does the world appear stable to you when you're looking at it? Why doesn't it appear as jerky and nauseating as the poorly filmed video? Here's why; your internal model (perception) operates under the assumption that the world outside is stable. Your eyes are not like video cameras, they simply venture out to find more details to feed into the internal model. They're not like camera lenses that you're seeing through, they're gathering bits of data to feed the world inside your skull. And that's what all of your senses are doing. Your senses are not like windows to objective reality, they're more like data-collecting devices that gather bits of information about a narrow spectrum of the outside world (whatever that is) in the form of sensory inputs and these inputs feed your internal model of reality in an active feedback loop. In other words, the reality you perceive, your brain is actively creating it. It is more accurate to say that everything that you perceive or what you call "Reality" is a specie-centric simplified interface designed to keep you alive. Your senses are not evolved to show you the objective reality (The Truth) they're designed to keep you alive. What we call reality doesn't exist anywhere except in the neurochemistry of our brains.

Note: Don't confuse my thought written above with "Solipsism" which is a philosophical notion that basically says nothing exists or nothing is real. Every concept I write has strong roots in science and must not be confused with philosophical opinions.

Purpose And Meaning

I've always wondered about the objective "Purpose" of life or existence itself, "If" there is any at all. And lately, I've started to realize that these questions; the purpose, and meaning of life might be the product of our cognitive models which are designed to operate under linear causality. Why must anything have a purpose? Why must anything have a meaning? What is meaning in the first place? Well, meaning arises from comparison, it thereby requires a conscious entity (such as humans) that's capable of comparison. The meaning will only exist for systems capable of comparing, outside of those narrow systems meaning doesn't exist neither do the words like "Purpose". And speaking of meaning, do you know that almost all ontologies and almost all physicists agree that reality is made of information. What is information? Information is meaning conveyed by symbolism as defined by the QGR research group. As we established above meaning is subjective and for meaning to even exist, it requires a system capable of comparison, or you could say a conscious system. If meaning doesn't exist without a conscious observer, by definition that means the information doesn't exist which, intern, means that reality doesn't exist because reality is made of information as suggested by modern physics. What that means is, reality doesn't exist until the conscious observer is present. This is also backed up by the "measurement problem" that resides at the heart of quantum mechanics... In this writing, I got distracted by the physics aspect of this topic. Anyway back to our topic... A universe without purpose should neither depress us nor suggest that our lives are purposeless. Through an awe-inspiring cosmic history, we find ourselves on this remote planet in a remote corner of the universe, endowed with intelligence and self-awareness. We should not despair, but should humbly rejoice in making the most of these gifts. As far as the subjective meanings & purposes of life that we manufacture or derive from the systems or patterns that we engage with, in the unfolding of this causal flow, they're the functions $[f(x)]$ of the type of systems and patterns that you engage with. Words like "Meaning" and "purpose" are specie-centric and emerge from the survival needs governed by fitness payoffs.

Chemistry Or Mysticism

Contrary to popular belief our experiences, perceptions, emotions & feelings most of the time have nothing to do with objective reality, they're mere constructs - an illusory show put on by the exquisite neurochemistry of the brain. For instance, You can give me the most religious person in the world & the extreme atheist in the world. I can take them into the lab & literally exchange their beliefs & in terms of believing, turn them into each other for 10-20 minutes. Please keep in mind by the above argument I'm just trying to point out how by activating specific circuits of the brain you can trigger different experiences & different perceptions in people. I am in no way implying anything about anyone's religion. Now, If an epileptic seizure is focused in a particular sweet spot in the temporal lobe, the effect is something like a cognitive seizure, marked by changes of personality, hyper-religiosity (an obsession with religion and feelings of religious certainty), hypergraphia (extensive writing on a subject, usually about religion), the false sense of an external presence, and, often, the hearing voices that are attributed to a God. Some fraction of history's people like self-claimed mystics and leaders may have had temporal lobe epilepsy... When brain activity is kindled in the right spot, people hear voices. If a physician prescribes an anti-epileptic medication, the seizures go away and the voices disappear but also the part of their perception that was based on axioms grounded in that epileptic seizure also disappears. Our perception of "reality"(whatever that means) depends on what our biology is up to.

The Human Mind

Free Will

When people (including experts) use the words like neurons firing, brain wiring, this part of the brain being responsible for this & that part for that, it gives the impression that the brain is like a linear machine made of different parts & wires. However, this is far from the truth. I want you to think of your brain as an ecosystem filled with throbbing 86 billion jellyfish sparking electricity at each other, trying to approach each other, interacting, pruning, arborizing, and communicating. Your thoughts, ideas, motor commands, and cognition are the symphonies that arise from this ecosystem. Contrary to popular belief brain is not binary. Any transition in your mind, for example, a new thought, a different understanding, a different perspective, etc doesn't happen by any binary sort of mechanism, it's not like jumping from point A to B, from previous thought to new thought, It's more like a turn of the bird flock or like aurora borealis, that smooth nonbinary, nonlinear transition. That's how feelings, and thoughts, float through the ether of our minds. When you understand your brain like this, then you know every day something new is possible. Every day you're a new version of yourself. Because the brain is nonlinear and dynamic. The stream of your thoughts & pattern of your decisions today is not just governed by events of today or yesterday only, when you were young or 10 years ago, or 5 years ago your brain construed axioms that can sneak their way to any thought or decision you'll make today. And the messed up thing is it'll all happen subconsciously, you'll think it's because of this or that (a present event maybe) but the actual reason won't be accessible to your conscious mind. Your brain is like a complex & vast forest, in this forest, your constructed axioms, thoughts & experiences are like seeds, you think they're relevant for a day or so before they disappear forever but these seeds after years when you've apparently forgotten about them grow as tall trees. To be honest, nothing is really lost in the landscape of your mind. And you can just experience the events of this landscape but none of it is in your control, you just feel it is. And that, My fellow earthlings! Is the illusion of free will. The notion of choice, freewill is an illusory show put on by the exquisite neurochemistry of your brain.